AF300686

PREVENTING ABSENTEEISM AT WORK

Understand and beat this widespread phenomenon

Written by Célestin de Meeûs
Translated by Emma Hanna

Coaching 50MINUTES.com

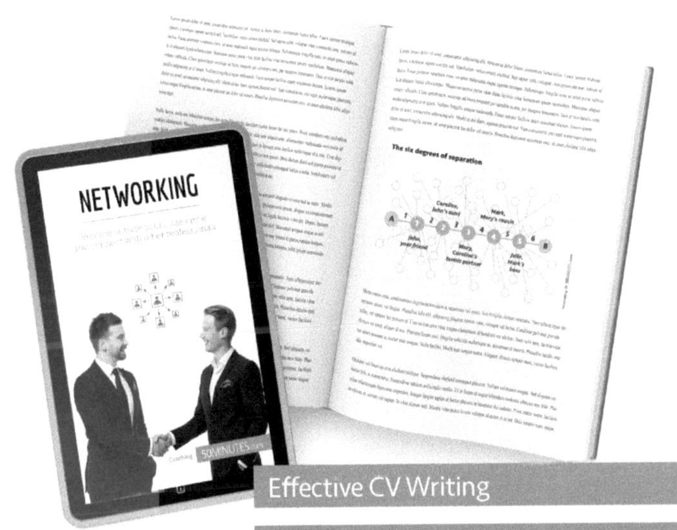

PREVENTING ABSENTEEISM AT WORK

- **Problem:** how can you combat absenteeism, which is becoming an increasingly widespread problem in the world of work?
- **Uses:** creating a healthier work environment by understanding the underlying factors that affect workers' wellbeing.
- **Professional context:** human resources, professional psychology, work-life balance, employee satisfaction.
- **FAQs:**
  - What is absenteeism?
  - How should I react to an absentee colleague?
  - How can I broach this subject with my colleagues?
  - What personal image do I project when I do not attend work?
  - Are crackdowns a good solution?
  - What does the law say?

Entire generations before us have fought long

and hard to secure the right to a dignified, healthy working environment. Even though it may seem as though that battle was won long ago, there are still certain social demands which can gradually lead to professional alienation. Raising and caring for a family, providing your children with an education, providing for their financial and emotional needs, paying your debts, taking holidays, and so on, are all needs or responsibilities which can quickly become overwhelming. Generally, these elements, plus a loving partner who shares your values and lifestyle, are seen as the necessary ingredients for a happy, fulfilling life. But this happiness comes at a price: work.

Although our society is based on an economy which is self-regulated by the law of supply and demand, it has not yet learned how to listen to the working population which is now expressing its increasing dissatisfaction with the system that it has participated in until now through the skyrocketing percentage of the population that suffers from depression.

The figures vary greatly by country, but in Belgium, for example, they are alarming: the absentee rate is constantly increasing, and rose from 5.95% in 2012 to 6.26% in 2014. However, it is also necessary to consider the professional context that gives rise to this situation. For example, we need to consider whether or not human resources departments are providing adequate solutions, if employees could benefit from psychological help, and how we should take work-life balance and employee satisfaction into account.

The phenomenon of absenteeism reflects a general sentiment that it is time for change, because the only way to create a fairer, more harmonious society is by working together to forge it, instead of expecting it to appear out of nowhere. As such, we need to try to understand the factors and motivations which drive so many people to express their dissatisfaction through absenteeism, in order to identify an effective way to combat this ever-more relevant trend.

UNDERSTANDING ABSENTEEISM: THE BASICS

ALARMING TRENDS

All capitalist countries are affected by absenteeism. Of course, the situations in Great Britain and the United States differ significantly from those in, for example, France and Belgium because of the differences in the attitudes and behaviours typical of those countries. However, there is one particular factor which is a driving force behind absenteeism in any country: stress.

Absentee rates do not just vary by country, but also by sector (public vs. private), role, and so on.

In the UK

Sickness absence has actually seen a fairly steady overall decrease in the UK in the past 20 years. While workers lost an average of 7.2 working days per year to sickness absence in 1993, this fell to 4.3 days in 2016, the lowest rate on record. Absentee rates are highest for employees aged 50-64.

In the United States

Absenteeism is a much rarer problem on the other side of the Atlantic. In 2014, the average absentee rate was 2.2% for men and 3.8% for women; in both cases, absenteeism was highest among senior citizens (those aged 50+).

In France

In 2013, official statistics showed that there was tremendous variation in absentee rates according to region and sector. The South-East had the highest rate, with an average of 23.6 days absent, compared to the South-West with an average of 14.3 days. The sectors with the highest absentee rates were: transport (with an average of 24.7 days absent per person per year), followed by healthcare (21.5 days absent), commerce (16.7 days), services (15.4 days), industry (12.5 days) and construction (10.8 days).

In Belgium

Belgium's absentee rate has been steadily increasing since 2008. According to a study carried out by *Securex*, a Belgian organisation which specialises in human resources, long-term absenteeism is actually growing at a constant rate. In 2014, just over 6% of workers were absent every day. These absentee workers provided a wide variety of reasons for their absences, from illness and workplace injuries to sabbaticals and daily delays.

GENERAL OBSERVATION

A common trend in each of the countries analysed was that the average age of the working population (which is constantly increasing) has an undeniable effect on absentee rates.

UNDERLYING CAUSES

Average age of the working population

The baby-boomers (the generation born just after the end of the Second World War, i.e. between

1947 and 1965) is approaching retirement age, which has led to an inevitable increase in the average age of the working population. According to the same study by *Securex*, individuals aged 50 or more accounted for 20% of Belgium's working population, which represented an increase of 7% since 2012. Given that age is an important factor for an individual's overall health, it often influences how much time employees take off: although older workers take time off less frequently, their absences due to illness tend to last longer.

On average, baby-boomers racked up 7.6 times more days absent than their younger colleagues. As such, they account for 15.9% of long-term absenteeism and 2.7% of short-term absenteeism. In other words, the under-50s are absent more frequently, but for shorter periods of time.

The financial crisis

The fact that employees sometimes lose motivation when working for an economy that seems doomed is a factor that cannot be ignored. When money is tight and working harder yields fewer results, this creates a breeding ground for pressure and stress.

Overwork

Many employees are used to giving not just 100%, but 110% on a daily basis in order to increase their income. This situation fuels both stress and anxiety, and drives many people to burnout. In Europe, stress is actually responsible for 30% of absenteeism. For example, in the UK, the total cost of stress is estimated to be the equivalent of £56 per employee per day.

According to American studies, the main cause of absenteeism on the other side of the Atlantic is harassment and intimidation, while burnout and stress take second place. As such, it is unsurprising that American preventative measures tend to focus primarily on the worker's physical wellbeing. In fact, 800 000 Americans have taken up cardiac coherence, a technique designed to combat stress, in which the patient is hooked up to a computer and uses breathing exercises to try to lower their heart rate.

REASONS FOR ABSENCES

Sickness absence

In Belgium, employees were absent for an average of 14.05 days each due to illness in 2013. Of course, no one can avoid catching the occasional virus and being left bedridden for a couple of days, but employers may wish to put measures in place to deal with prolonged sickness absences.

These measures have three aims:

- to verify that the employee is too ill to work and that the length of their absence is justified (based on a supporting medical certificate which should be submitted within a certain timeframe);
- to frame discussions about the employee's eventual return to work in a way that helps them reintegrate to a normal working environment;
- to provide assistance for the employee during the reintegration process and adapt their workload according to their needs.

The benefits of using this approach are twofold:

it reduces long-term absences by making them shorter, and reduces consultation fees by having medical checks organised in an appropriate healthcare centre. This benefits both the employer, who will be better informed about their employees, and the employee, who will feel that their needs are being met and their voice is being heard.

Workplace injuries

Fascinating differences can be observed between the situations in France and Belgium regarding workplace injuries, as the sectors which are most affected by workplace injuries in France correspond to the sectors which are least affected in Belgium, and vice versa. What are the reasons for these trends?

Although the Belgian transport and construction sectors have been shrinking consistently since 1985 due to the tightening of security regulations, these fields also have the highest absentee rates. However, in France, occupational health risk prevention policies which are much stricter than the Belgian equivalents have been put in place in the industrial and construction sectors.

On the contrary, the commercial and transport sectors, which have been more strongly affected by the crisis, have skimped on similar measures in an attempt to save money.

Sabbaticals

The practice of taking sabbaticals emerged during the 1980s. A sabbatical is a leave of absence taken by an employee during the course of their career. Sabbaticals are taken for a variety of reasons:

- returning to education;
- travelling;
- fulfilling a lifelong dream, etc.

For those who decide to take a temporary leave of absence, and who therefore fit into this category, it can be a very beneficial experience, as they will be able to return to their former position after their break and pick things up exactly where they left off. Over time, sabbaticals have become a kind of tacit agreement between employers and employees to maximise the quality of both the professional and personal lives of employees.

However, sabbaticals must not exceed a certain length of time. The maximum duration of a sabbatical varies by country, but generally speaking the limit is set at three to six months. Other types of leave can also be loosely grouped with this category, such as parental leave and leave to provide medical assistance (usually to care for a sick relative). The latter is the third most common cause of absenteeism in America.

Daily delays

Time spent stuck in traffic or lost due to public transport delays are considered daily delays. As a result, employees lose valuable time and in the long run this leads to significant losses for employers.

DID YOU KNOW?

In 2013 alone, absenteeism cost employers a total of €10.6 billion in Belgium. On average, a work day costs €160 per worker, without taking replacement costs and the negative effect on productivity into account.

IS PREVENTION THE SOLUTION?

These causes can however be easily avoided, particularly through the use of preventative measures. Companies have long used restrictive measures to combat absenteeism, but they do not seem to be effective. On the one hand, punishments are not a solution, and on the other hand, rewards (promotions or bonuses based on effort, etc.) do not seem to be effective either, in addition to being expensive. As such, companies are increasingly turning towards preventative measures.

A clinic in Liège (Belgium) is one of several organisations which have been holding test workshops which aim to bring a wide variety of managers together so that they can share their experiences and try to find solutions to combat this phenomenon.

Several ideas emerged from the sessions held in Liège, including:

- implement medical checks in order to reduce absences of more than two weeks;
- draw up a detailed report on absenteeism and

target the person or group of people who are most frequently absent in order to contain the problem more easily;
- analyse and try to understand the causes of the problem in order to improve the working environment;
- introduce training about absenteeism in order to:
  - facilitate employee reintegration after long absences;
  - prevent absenteeism;
  - reduce short-term absences;
  - open dialogue;
  - increase awareness and conscientiousness among managers and employees.

PROFESSIONAL WELLBEING

Stress is the number one cause of work-related problems, and is behind 37% of absences in Belgium. According to the Brussels newspaper *Métro* (24 September 2014), 97% of burnout cases in Belgium are work-related and, more specifically, are related to increasing productivity demands. The following symptoms are warning signs that you may be suffering from excessive stress:

- experiencing insomnia or palpitations;
- difficulty concentrating or headaches;
- sudden, excessive bursts of anger, or total apathy.

If all of these apply to you, it is very likely that you are suffering from excessive stress.

The Karpman drama triangle

According to the Karpman drama triangle, which was devised by the American psychologist Stephen B. Karpman, we unconsciously play games and adopt one of three roles in our relationships with others, particularly during times of conflict, unless we engage in more self-reflection. The possible roles we can adopt are those of a victim who is wounded by those in positions of greater strength, a persecutor who oppresses those in positions of greater vulnerability, and a rescuer. While victim-persecutor relationships can always be considered "lose-lose" relationships, the rescuer's role can lead to two different scenarios: for example, in the case of absenteeism the rescuer can either become a persecutor (by trying to combat absenteeism through a rewards system, which then makes the employee dependent on the employer's financial power), or they can act as a true rescuer and act in the collective interest of the company by introducing preventative measures.

VICTIM
"I have done nothing wrong"

RESCUER
"I want to help"

PERSECUTOR
"I can do whatever I want"

PRACTICAL EXERCISE

If you see yourself in one of these roles, it is not too late to adjust your behaviour! Next time you find yourself in a similar situation, identify which of these roles you fall into and distance yourself from it.

- Be honest with others and with yourself.
- Respect yourself and others will respect you.
- Be diplomatic: negotiate to find the best possible solution.
- It is never a bad idea to show your sense of humour and take things a bit less seriously.

If you are experiencing near-constant stress, it is essential to work up the courage to talk to your team about it. Talk to your colleagues and your superiors before the situation can overwhelm you, because feeling more confident in your work will make you a more productive, flexible and innovative employee.

TOP TIPS

To discern whether or not your work environment is having a negative impact on your health, start by asking yourself the following questions:

- Are you often tense at work?
- Is work often on your mind in the evenings?
- Do you have enough time to devote to your hobbies?
- How do you cope with the need to be available at all times?
- Do you feel that people listen to you?
- Are you able to say no?
- Are you being bullied?
- Can you speak to your superiors when you have a problem?
- Do you feel valued by your colleagues?
- Are you given enough independence?

There are many ways of solving these kinds of problems.

- If you are an employee, it may be a good idea to:

  - ◦ take the time to write a to-do list;
  - ◦ learn to keep things in perspective;
  - ◦ listen to your colleagues and friends;
  - ◦ speak to those around you;
  - ◦ dare to make your dreams a reality!
- If you are an employer, it is advisable to do all you can to:
  - ◦ motivate your employees by ensuring that they know the purpose of their work;
  - ◦ give them independence and responsibilities;
  - ◦ encourage an atmosphere of solidarity by honing each employee's skills and putting their talents to good use;
  - ◦ reduce the physical and emotional burden placed on your employees;
  - ◦ create more part-time positions.

Avoid the following pitfalls:

- bottling things up and letting your frustration fester;
- assuming that things will automatically get better with time;
- letting yourself be overwhelmed by overwork;
- adopting the role of a victim, a persecutor or a rescuer.

By keeping this advice in mind, you will observe a new kind of relationship emerging – not a "win-lose" relationship, but rather, a respectful, honest "win-win" relationship between employer and employee. In the end, the key to ensuring the wellbeing of everyone lies in communication, during the good times and the bad.

FAQS

WHAT IS ABSENTEEISM?

Absenteeism refers to a tendency to be absent from work. This can be caused by poor wellbeing which can be avoided through preventative measures, improving the work environment and improved working relationships. It is often the result of the sensation of being physically or psychologically trapped in the workplace. On a deeper level, it is the manifestation of a feeling of alienation in the workplace which is caused by employer-employee conflict.

HOW SHOULD I REACT TO AN AB-SENTEE COLLEAGUE?

If one of your colleagues begins to take frequent absences, try to put yourself in their shoes and get inside their head. Ask yourself what might be causing them to neglect their work.

In order to support them, it is important to:

- know yourself so that you can tackle problems effectively;
- open a dialogue with your colleague;
- remind them that work should never be the cause of such alienation or frustration that setting foot there seems like an insurmountable task;
- help them to understand that work should, above all, be a path to increased wellbeing;
- create an environment of mutual support by assigning responsibilities more efficiently, according to each person's talents and abilities.

HOW CAN I BROACH THIS SUBJECT WITH MY COLLEAGUES?

Even though we are constantly stressing the importance of dialogue and communication, it can still be difficult to approach a colleague and start a conversation about our issues, especially when this could lead them to pity us. This means that we need to find a way to overcome this obstacle.

Finding the right balance is just a matter of trust. Once you find a colleague whom you trust and who is willing to lend a listening ear, tell them about what you are going through – perhaps even outside of work, to make things easier – and express how you feel, so that you can let your frustration out and feel heard, understood and unburdened.

Furthermore, given that work makes our personal lives better by improving our wellbeing, it is important that the reverse is equally true, and that our personal lives are structured in a way that allows us to thrive at work.

WHAT PERSONAL IMAGE DO I PROJECT WHEN I DO NOT ATTEND WORK?

Absentees often worry about the message it sends their colleagues when they are unable to work – will it cast them in a better light or, on the contrary, will it cause their professional relationships to deteriorate? All the evidence suggests that our colleagues do not particularly enjoy having to take on the responsibilities of someone who takes long, frequent leaves of absence for no good reason (in their opinion).

The question then becomes: how can we remedy this situation when our personal or professional issues become more and more pressing and increasingly prevent us from attending work? These problems cannot always be solved easily, so we need to at least try to dispel social pressure by learning to distance ourselves from our image. After all, our image is not the real problem: it is our unhappiness and poor wellbeing. Remember that while it is important to keep things in perspective, it is just as important to trust, communicate, know yourself and admit it when you have difficulties, as this is the only way to find a solution.

ARE CRACKDOWNS A GOOD SOLUTION?

Definitely not. As we saw in the section on preventative measures, neither the carrot nor the stick is an effective long-term strategy for dealing with the problem. Punishments will alienate employees, while rewards are too expensive. This is why other solutions have been suggested, including preventative measures. This approach reminds workers that they are not just a cog in an anonymous, impersonal machine, and that they have a vital role to play.

In order to implement an effective system of preventative measures which suits your company's needs, human resources managers can:

- create forums where problems can be addressed directly in order to find solutions;
- amend workplace rules to include legal measures which protect and/or punish behaviours like absenteeism, and keep employees informed of these amendments;
- keep a file which records of the numbers of absences, the reasons for them, and related checks so that the problem can be analysed effectively and solutions can be found.

WHAT DOES THE LAW SAY?

Instead of bottling up any frustrations with your job, which will leave you unable to thrive professionally, learn about your rights and try not to use frequent absences as a coping mechanism for the unhappiness your work is causing you. Legal frameworks are in place to protect workers (such as Belgium's law of 28 February 2014, which addresses employee wellbeing and psychological risk factors), so it is best to find alternative ways of coping.

In fact, if your employer learns that you have been taking time off frequently, they will not hesitate to use their own rights to try and solve the problem in their own way. Instead of improving the situation, these kinds of legal measures usually widen the rift between you and your company, leading to misunderstandings, frustration and a loss of respect which can prove destructive on both sides.

Case study: Belgium

In Belgium, a law was enacted on 28 February 2014, building on a law dating from 4 August 1996 regarding employee wellbeing while on the job. The amendments included the following points:

- Previously, the idea of psychological risk factors was exclusively focused on preventing violence, bullying and sexual harassment in the workplace. Now, however, the law stipulates that companies must take psychological risk factors into account when drawing up the company's preventative policy, just like the other

risks which threaten workers' health and
safety.

- The creation of the post of a prevention
  advisor, who provides information, gui-
  dance and a listening ear for all of the
  company's employees.
- Each prevention advisor must undergo
  a minimum of five days of training, in
  addition to an annual monitoring session.
  Their aims are to make employers aware
  of the underlying causes of absenteeism,
  to help employees to prevent absence,
  etc.
- Individual requests which fall into a collective framework will be dealt with more
  quickly.
- The results of any monitoring or inspec-
  tions regarding wellbeing in the workplace
  must be made public.
- Any employee who is targeted by violent
  behaviour, bullying or sexual harassment
  has the right to claim a lump sum from
  the labour tribunal as compensation for
  the physical and/or psychological harm
  inflicted on them.

Through this law, employees and employers have gained rights based on mutual respect. As the laws get tougher, both sides are becoming more conscientious.

OVER TO YOU

- Are you often tense at work? Take a step back and do not be afraid to let your sense of humour shine through.
- Do you find yourself obsessing over your work at night? Try out cardiac coherence as a way of relaxing, and learn to separate your personal and professional lives.
- Do you feel like you have to be available at all times? Dare to say no, and switch off your phone for a few hours so that you can make the most of the present and its peace and quiet.
- Do you have enough time to devote to your hobbies? If not, speak to your superiors, learn to manage your time, and take time for yourself to relax.
- Do people listen to you? Communication is vital, so share your frustrations with your friends and colleagues before they overwhelm you.

- Are you able to say no? Take the bull by the horns and assert your rights. Read up on the law and how it protects you.
- Do you feel valued? Think back to Karpman's triangle. Do you value your colleagues? Try not to go on the defensive; break this vicious circle and distance yourself from it, without adopting the role of a victim, a rescuer or a persecutor any longer. Be diplomatic, believe in yourself and raise the issue in a conversation. Learn to respect yourself and others will respect you.
- Do you have enough independence? Make your own decisions, and tell your superiors about your best ideas.

In summary, dare to make your dreams a reality.

ADVICE FOR EMPLOYERS

- Do your employees seem lost? It is up to you to motivate them. Explain the purpose of their work, and the value they bring to the company.
- Do they need more independence? You can provide this by giving them more responsibilities and explaining things clearly. Remember, a happier employee is a more productive,

creative employee.

- Is your company plagued by absenteeism? Restrictive measures do not work; neither punishments nor rewards are effective in the long term. Aim to use preventative measures and training, but remember that you also have legal measures at your disposal that can be used if necessary.
- Creating a sense of solidarity within the company is essential, as this will hone each employee's skills. Make optimal use of individual talents.
- Do your employees seem tired? If so, reducing the physical and emotional toll of their work is essential – when their physical health takes a hit, this will have a knock-on effect on their emotional health, and will quickly lead to burnout.
- Breathe fresh life into your company by increasing the number of part-time positions available.

Remember that you, too, can make your dream a way of contributing to the collective good.

We want to hear from you!
Leave a comment on your online library
and share your favourite books on social media!

FURTHER READING

BIBLIOGRAPHY

- Berger, S. (2005) S'offrir une année sabbatique. *La Libre Belgique*. [Online]. [Accessed 12 October 2017]. Available from: <http://www.lalibre.be/economie/libre-entreprise/s-offrir-une-annee-sabbatique-51b88b31e4b0de6db9ac8e4a>

- Comer, M. (2017) Sickness absence in the labour market: 2016. *Office for National Statistics.* [Online]. [Accessed 12 October 2017]. Available from: <https://www.ons.gov.uk/employmentandlabourmarket/peopleinwork/labourproductivity/articles/sicknessabsenceinthelabourmarket/2016>

- Eurogip. (2014) *Points statistiques AT-MP Belgique. Données 2005-2012.* [Online]. [Accessed 12 October 2017]. Available from: <http://www.eurogip.fr/images/documents/3639/Eurogip_92F.pdf>

- Mensura Belgique. (No date) *Des solutions aux problèmes d'absentéisme dans votre entreprise.* [Online]. [Accessed 12 October 2017]. Available from: <https://www.mensurakinderbijslag.be/uploads/media/54f9b73eb394f.pdf?antaresab2ecde>

- Service public fédéral. Emploi, Travail et Concertation sociale Belgique. (2014) *Nouvelle législation relatives aux risques psychosociaux au travail à partir du 1er septembre 2014.* [Online]. [Accessed 12 October 2017]. Available from: <http://www.emploi.belgique.be/defaultNews.aspx?id=41483>

ADDITIONAL SOURCES

- *Eurostat* website: <http://ec.europa.eu/eurostat>
- *Forbes* website: <http://www.forbes.com>
- *FranceTVinfo* website: <http://www.francetvinfo.fr>
- *HRworld* website: <http://www.hrworld.be>
- *La Libre Belgique* website: <http://www.lalibre.be>
- *Le Figaro* website: <http://www.lefigaro.fr>
- *LeVif L'Express* website: <http://www.levif.be>
- *Mensura* website: <http://www.mensura.be/homePage.aspx>
- *Office for National Statistics* (UK) website: <http://www.ons.gov.uk>
- *sdworx* website: <http://www.sdworx.be>
- *Securex* website: <http://www.securex.be>
- *US Bureau of Labor Statistics* website: <http://www.bls.gov>
- *Wolters Kluwer* website: <http://wolterskluwer.com>

IMPROVE YOUR GENERAL KNOWLEDGE

IN A BLINK OF AN EYE !

www.50minutes.com

Although the editor makes every effort to verify the accuracy of the information published, 50Minutes.com accepts no responsibility for the content of this book.

www.50minutes.com

Ebook EAN: 9782808004862

Paperback EAN: 9782808006026

Legal Deposit: D/2017/12603/840

Cover: © Primento

Digital conception by Primento, the digital partner of publishers.